KIM AND THE

Cover still shows, from
and Simon Turner as

Cover still by courtesy of Beta Film GmbH & Co., Munich.

KIM AND THE BURIED TREASURE
The second in a series

Also available:

KIM THE DETECTIVE

Jens K. Holm

Kim and the Buried Treasure

Futura Publications Limited
A Contact Book

A Contact Book

First published in Great Britain in 1975
by Futura Publications Limited, in association
with Arthur Barker Limited

ISBN 0 8600 7226 6

Printed in Great Britain by
Cox & Wyman Ltd
London, Reading and Fakenham

Futura Publications Limited
110 Warner Road
London SE5

First filmed in Great Britain by Antrobus Films Ltd
as an Antrobus/Taurus co-production

A 10 part BBC television series entitled KIM & CO

Chapter 1

I thought I could hear footsteps behind me. I stopped to listen, but unfortunately at that very moment I trod on a twig.

The twig cracked, with a noise which I felt was loud enough to be heard all over the wood. It was very dark; you could see bits of the sky in between the tree tops, but there were no stars. The last few days had been very hot, and now a storm was brewing. Dark, heavy clouds lowered threateningly, and there was an odd feeling of tension in the air.

I stood quite still, holding my breath. But all I could hear was the thudding of my own heart. I took a couple of steps forward and collided with a tree. What on earth was the matter with me? I wasn't usually nervous in the wood at night!

Now, take it easy, I told myself, just take

it easy! I pulled myself together and groped my way back to the narrow path. After all, I knew this part of the wood, didn't I? In a minute or so I'd be at the big oak tree where I was to meet the others. I walked on, swinging the lantern from my hand. I would rather have liked to light it, but on the other hand I felt safer in the dark. It was a real lantern, the old-fashioned kind, with a handle: the sort of thing pirates used in the old days. I'd found it in a corner of my uncle's attic and brought it along this evening, thinking it would be just the thing for what we were planning to do.

All of a sudden something whipped into my face. I was so frightened that I broke out in a cold sweat and gave a muffled shriek. Only then did I realize it was just a branch. I tell you I felt a right Charlie! I picked up the lantern, which I'd dropped, and went on, keeping my eyes on the tree tops. That's the best way to make sure you don't get lost in a dark wood. There had been quite a strong wind earlier in the day, but it had died down now, and everything was still. The leaves hung motionless from the branches. There wasn't a sound to be heard. I just wished the storm would hurry up and break.

As I was thinking this, I heard the footsteps again. There was no doubt about it this time. I stopped. Yes, there really *was* someone walking right behind me.

Then I realized what a fool I was! It could easily be one of the others arriving rather early, the same as me. It might be Erik, or Specs, or equally well it could be Katya, and they could have decided, for some obscure reason, to come along this path, even though there were quicker ways for them to get to the meeting place. Yes, of course it must be one of them – and perhaps he or she was just as frightened as I was! Whoever it was had stopped at the same moment as me. I took a long, deep breath, and started hooting like an owl. That's our signal.

It was not a particularly successful hoot; I don't suppose any self-respecting owl would have been taken in for a moment, but it was the best I could manage. While I hooted I was busy persuading myself there was nothing at all to be frightened of. I expected to hear an answering signal behind me any minute.

Finally I ran out of breath and stopped hooting . . .

. . . and behind me, quite close, I heard a man laugh. I was really frightened now, more frightened than I'd ever been in my life before. It was not a nice sort of laugh. It sounded mocking and sarcastic – the kind of laugh I'd only ever heard in horror films up till now. For a moment I was rooted to the spot with terror, and then I ran for my life, crashing through the trees and bushes, falling, scrambling up again, stumbling over roots. My one thought was to get away! I had no idea whereabouts in the wood I might be, or even if I was running in the right direction. Oddly enough, I was still clutching the lantern. I didn't give myself time to stop and listen, I just went stumbling on, and suddenly I found myself running straight into the stream.

At least I could tell roughly where I was now. I knew the stream; it ran quite close to the big oak, and I had only to follow it for a bit to get to our meeting place. I stood still for a moment, straining my ears for any sound of pursuit, but there was nothing to be heard. Then I dipped my hand in the icy water to find out which way the current was flowing. Reviewing the situation, I decided I'd have to turn left.

At first I thought the oak would be some way off, but suddenly I found myself on the spot. I'd half hoped to find the others there already, but I was disappointed. There was no one else there. I sat down under the old oak and stared into the darkness, feeling very lonely, and listening for footsteps the whole time. It was all very odd. Who was the man? And what on earth was he doing here in the wood in the middle of the night?

Something moved, quite close to me, and I jumped. But this time there was no cause for alarm. It was only a hedgehog. The hedgehog came slowly and suspiciously closer, and took a good sniff at me. I put out my hand and touched it. It rolled up and stayed perfectly still, just a ball of prickles. Suddenly I felt all right, and not afraid of anything in the world. This was what I'd been wanting the whole time, just what I needed: another living creature! It's funny how it steadies you, having something else alive around the place, anything – a puppy or even a hedgehog, so long as it's alive.

I put the lantern down on the ground and relaxed. I felt quite ready to face the others now, in fact I really had to laugh at myself for taking fright like that!

I leaned back against the tree trunk and thought. Five days had passed since Erik,

Katya and I buried our treasure in the wood, near the hut we had built. And now, once we'd all met, we were going to go back to the place together and dig the treasure up again. I thought how surprised Specs would be when he saw all that money! Specs still didn't know anything about our treasure; we hadn't told him about the thousand *kroner* which we intended to use for his invention. I couldn't wait to see his face when he found out.

However, I'd better explain who we are, in case you don't know already. First there's Erik, who will soon be fifteen. His hair is fair in winter and practically white in summer. He's been my best friend for years. We're in the same class at school in Copenhagen, and during the holidays we live quite close to each other in this little fishing village and seaside resort on the north coast of Zealand, Erik with his parents and me with my uncle and aunt. They live here all the time, and I visit them every summer. Specs, whose real name is Palle and who is in our class too, was spending the summer here for the first time. His parents aren't all that rich, in fact his father was out of work for quite a time, and his mother's been very ill. This year (on doctor's orders, I think) they'd rented a house here for the summer, the old brown bungalow behind the birch trees, the one with the garage. Specs never mentions it, but it must have been difficult for his parents to scrape up enough money for the holiday. (My own parents aren't exactly millionaires either, but then *my* holidays here don't cost me anything. Erik's father, on the other hand, is quite well off.) Well, that's about it. Oh, I'd better add that at first Erik and I weren't too pleased to find that Specs was spending the summer holidays here too. We weren't friends of his at school; in fact you could say we thought him a pretty pathetic figure. All he knows about is physics and chemistry, but he's mad keen on them, and since both subjects are a positive nightmare to me and Erik, you can see that we didn't have much in common. At least, so we thought at the beginning of the holidays, but we soon found out that we had quite the wrong idea about Specs. When you get to know him better, he's a good mate.

Specs has made himself a laboratory in the empty garage of the bungalow, where he runs up everything you can possibly think of, and a lot you probably can't.

That's all about Specs. And now a word or so about Katya. I suppose it doesn't look very polite of me to put the only girl among us last, but that's because I'm not quite sure what to say about her. Well, here goes: she's fourteen, she has dark hair and brown, tanned skin, and she's very pretty. Her father is Russian or Polish or something of that sort; he's a political refugee, and he's only just got a provisional permit to stay in Denmark. Katya lives with him and does the cooking and looks after the house, but all the same she manages to spend nearly all day with us. Perhaps that's because her father is a professor, and professors don't mind so much about the house getting dusted properly. And Katya says he prefers being alone. Katya herself speaks fluent Danish, because she's lived in Denmark for five years. With relations of some sort, I think. But her father has only just come to this country, so he doesn't speak Danish so well. When you hear Katya talk, there's only a very slight accent – I like it, myself – to show that she wasn't born here.

Personally, I think Katya is the nicest, funniest, prettiest girl I've ever met; I always used to think girls were a nuisance and spoilt everything, but I don't mind admitting I was wrong!

Reading this part I've just written may have been a bit boring, but at least it's over now. Oh, no – there's one more thing I should add: Specs had thought up a new kind of carburettor or something, with a bit of help from old Stoffer (whose real name is Mr Christoffersen, and who has a garage here in the village), and he wanted to try his invention out and see how it worked in practice, so as to work on the technical details. I also forgot something else: Erik has a dog called Schnapp. It wouldn't be right to leave Schnapp out, because according to him he's very much one of us.

However, back to the night in the wood. There I was, sitting in the dark with my back up against the old oak tree, waiting for the others and thinking about this and that. In about five minutes' time I heard quick, light footsteps coming along the path. I grabbed the lantern, in case of emergencies, and prepared to make a quick getaway if necessary. However, it wasn't necessary; in a moment I heard the owl's hoot, and at once I replied the same way.

'Hi, Katya!' I called. I'd recognized her voice, 'Too-whit, too-whoo!'

'Too-whit, too-whoo! Hullo. Why on earth are you sitting here in the dark?'

'Oh, I thought I'd save the lantern till later,' I said evasively. 'Did you come on your own?'

'Yes, I thought I'd be late. I had to slip out of the back door.'

'You shouldn't go wandering round the wood at night by yourself,' I told her.

'Why not? What is there to be afraid of? Why do the rest of you always think I must be a coward just because I'm a girl? *You* aren't frightened, so why should I be?'

'Hmm!' I said, clearing my throat. At the moment I felt I'd rather not tell her about the mysterious man in the wood.

'Well, actually I *was* a bit frightened,' she admitted, honestly. 'I was relieved when I heard you here already.'

I lit the lantern and put it down on the grass, and we sat down and waited.

We hardly said anything, and when we did speak it was in whispers. The wood was so quiet that you could hardly bring yourself to talk out loud. But even apart from that, I couldn't think of anything much to say. Katya and I had plenty to talk about when we were with the others, but somehow as soon as we were on our own, just the two of us, we'd fall silent. Perhaps it wasn't really that we couldn't think of anything to say; we just preferred not to talk. In spite of that, I enjoyed being with Katya.

Anyway, in a moment we heard a sound like a herd of wild elephants stampeding through the wood. Now and then the herd stopped, hooted like an owl, and then stampeded on, coming closer and closer.

'Here come Specs and Erik!' said Katya, chuckling.

'You just possibly could be right,' I said dryly, giving an answering hoot, and a few moments later the other two arrived.

'Hi! Have you been waiting long?'

'Well, not very. Let's get a move on now.'

I went on ahead, with the lantern. The path was so narrow that we had to walk in single file. Erik came behind me, followed by Katya, with Specs bringing up the rear. As we went along I was thinking that of course we could have dug the treasure up in daytime. Which would have been considerably easier and more convenient. On the other hand, I don't remember ever reading about anyone doing a thing like that in broad daylight, given half a chance to do it at dead of night, by the light of a lantern, and surrounded by dangers. So here we were, walking along the path, and I think we all felt it was a very solemn occasion. After all, this was not just a game! There really *was* a treasure buried in the ground, a hundred paces from the door of our hut and forty-eight paces from the stunted tree. We could always have put the money in a savings account, I suppose, but I'm sure you will agree that it would have been a very boring thing to do with a thousand *kroner*.

At last we arrived. The clearing in front of our hut was in darkness, but as we stepped into it the first flash of lightning crossed the sky, and almost immediately there was a loud clap of thunder, followed by the first few raindrops.

I was feeling good. This was just the sort of weather for the occasion! Erik seemed to feel much the same – at all events, he was grinning all over his face. He went into the hut and came out again, carrying the spade.

'OK, then, let's get down to work! Kim, you pace out the distance from the stunted tree, and I'll start over here by the hut. I have to make for the roots of that fallen tree over there, don't I? I wish I could see them, that's all!'

Katya picked the lantern up and took it over. 'Watch where you're going!' she cried. 'Look, I'll prop the lantern up on the tree roots here, and then you can see your way.'

Myself, I started walking from the stunted tree, and counted out forty-eight paces, going straight towards the three tall birch trees. You couldn't miss them; their sharp, black outlines stood out against the sky. There was another flash of lightning. Erik and I both kept going, but the lightning dazzled us, and we collided.

'This must be the place! Come over here, Katya.'

Katya was already on her way, carrying the lantern. We put it down on the ground, and marked a circle in the earth with our feet. Erik picked up the spade and handed it to Specs. The thunder rolled overhead. When the noise had died away, Erik made a short speech.

'Ladies and gentlemen – well, er, all I have to say, Specs, is that we didn't tell you about this before because ... er ... that is ... I mean to say ... well, we wanted to surprise you, see? And ... er ... um ... well, I bet you *will* be surprised! Now, start digging here, and see what you find. And if you do find anything, well, it's for your invention! Actually this is all Kim's doing, and it's his idea too. Katya and I only helped with the digging and keeping it a secret and all that. Right, dig away!'

At the same moment as Erik finished his speech the rain came down, and in a moment we were all wet to the skin. Specs stood there, quite still, the spade in his hand and a very foolish, puzzled expression on his face. I suppose he was wondering whether this was a practical joke. However, then he gave us a broad grin and drove the spade into the earth.

There was another flash of lightning, which came down somewhere in the wood this time. I thought of my aunt and uncle. I only hoped they wouldn't discover I was out in this storm. Specs was digging away busily now, and finally we heard the sound we were waiting for: the spade meeting the tin which contained the thousand *kroner*.

Specs bent down and picked it up out of the hole. 'But it's only a tin!' he said, in surprise.

'Try taking the lid off,' I suggested.

He did so, very carefully, as if he

thought there might be a poisonous snake inside. He looked at our faces, to see if we were laughing at him, and then held the tin up to the light and looked inside.

'It's empty,' he said, puzzled.

'Wh-what?' stammered Erik. 'Here, let's have a proper look!'

Specs handed me the tin. There was another flash of lightning, which gave me a clear view of the shiny interior of the tin.

'Specs is right,' I said slowly. 'It *is* empty!'

Chapter 2

It was still raining cats and dogs outside the hut, and large, heavy drops of water were dripping from several parts of the roof. We had sat down on the floor in a circle, the lantern in the middle. Its flame looked bright and cheerful. I'd put the empty tin on the ground beside it. Ourselves, we were wet, frozen, and very depressed.

'Look, do you mean to say you really put a thousand *kroner* in that tin before you buried it?' asked Specs. 'I mean, you're not just trying to make me think so for a joke, are you?'

'Do we look as if we thought it was a joke?' asked Erik in an injured tone. 'Of course we put the money in the tin. Ten brand new hundred *kroner* notes, just the way Kim got them from the bank, and I wish he'd left them there!'

'You thought burying them was a good idea too,' I growled.

'Did I? Well, you may be right, but I don't think so now. In fact I think it was about the silliest thing we've ever done! The money's gone, and you needn't think we'll ever get the crook that pinched it. No, it's goodbye to that money for keeps!'

'Couldn't we report it to the police?' asked Katya.

'Oh, don't be silly!' said Erik crossly.

'You shut up!' I snapped at him. 'Still, Katya, he's right – I don't think we could tell the police. Well, of course, we *could*, only I don't see much point in it. They'd just think we were round the bend, and everyone would fall about laughing, and we *still* wouldn't catch the thief because . . .'

'Yes, yes, all right!' Katya interrupted me. 'But who *is* the thief? Apart from us three, no one knew where we'd buried the tin – no one even knew there was a tin at all! Specs himself didn't know till this evening. How could the thief have found out? *I* didn't breathe a word to anyone, not even my father! I promise, I haven't said a word to a single person in the whole world!'

I saw that there were tears in her eyes; she sounded as if we were accusing her of giving the secret away, which we weren't doing at all! I know people always say that girls can't keep a secret, and no doubt that was why Katya seemed so afraid we'd blame her now. Personally, I think sweeping statements like that are a load of old rubbish.

'No one said you *did* say a word!' Erik snapped at her. 'And *I* didn't say a word to anyone either, and I bet Kim didn't – well, you didn't, Kim, did you?'

'Of course not,' I said. 'I was silent as the grave. We were *all* silent as the grave ... but all the same the thief found the spot and dug up our tin, pinched the money and buried the tin again ...'

'With our own spade!' interrupted Erik. 'Wait till I get my hands on him!'

'There's only one explanation,' said Specs. 'He must have been watching when you buried the tin.'

'That doesn't sound quite right,' said Katya thoughtfully. 'Who'd go prowling about the wood in the middle of the night just to watch *us*?'

'Yes, it does sound funny,' I agreed. 'No one ever comes here usually, even in the daytime. So suppose someone was here in the wood, then – well, I mean, he must have been here for some reason. Otherwise, like Katya says, people just don't go creeping around woods in the middle of the night. They might go for a stroll at the edge of the wood, maybe, but not right in here among the trees.'

'Perhaps someone followed us,' suggested Erik.

'But why, for goodness' sake? That's a rotten idea!'

'Yes, I'm inclined to agree with you!'

'We just don't have a single clue to give us a lead,' Specs said.

'Wait a minute – we may have a clue after all,' I said slowly. 'There was a man following me earlier this evening, when I was on my way to the oak tree. At first I thought it was one of you, so I stopped and hooted like an owl. And then – then he gave a horrible laugh.'

'So would I, if I heard you trying to hoot like an owl,' said Erik nastily.

'Oh, lay off, will you? It really was a horrible laugh, not a nice laugh at all. It was creepy – all mocking and sarcastic. Like in a horror film.'

'Like this?' asked Erik, laughing like Boris Karloff.

'Something like that!'

'Were you frightened?' asked Katya sympathetically.

'No, I was not!'

'Could you see him?' asked Erik. 'Would you know him again if you met him?'

'Not a chance. I didn't see him at all, I only heard him. Then I began to run, to throw him off my track. No, I know I wouldn't recognize him if I met him – not unless he laughed like that again.'

'Maybe he will, when he sees you!' said Erik. 'Well, that answers one question. He must have been the man who pinched our money.'

'You can't know for certain. Anyway, how do we go about finding him again? And even if we do find him, how do we go about getting our money back?'

'He must be the thief. It's obvious!' Erik repeated. 'So let's find him first, and then think about recovering the money.'

'It's stopped raining,' Specs informed us. 'Why not go and see if we can find any footprints or other clues now, before we go home? We can come out here again and have a thorough search tomorrow, when it's light, but I still think we ought to have a quick look now, with the lantern.'

Soon afterwards, we were all crawling around in front of our hut on hands and knees, searching the grass. But we found nothing.

'It's only in books that criminals leave all sorts of stuff lying about, so the detectives can get on their trail,' said Specs, prosaically. 'At all events, *our* thief hasn't lost so much as a button.'

'How about finger-prints?'

'Hey, that's not a bad idea! If he really did use our spade to dig up the money, he may have left finger-prints on some of the things in the hut. I don't know just how you take finger-prints, but I can find out by tomorrow,' Specs promised.

I didn't doubt it for a moment. When it comes to anything technical, in particular anything to do with physics or chemistry, there aren't many boys who can compete with Specs. And not many grown-ups either, come to that.

At the moment it looked as if our search was leading us nowhere. We were just about to give up and go home when Katya suddenly cried out, 'Hi, you lot, bring the lantern over here, quick! I think there's a piece of paper here.'

When we took a closer look at the object in question, it turned out to be on empty, crumpled cigarette packet. It was not lying in the middle of the clearing outside the hut, but right at the edge, half hidden by the undergrowth. The packet had once held twenty Broadways.

'Did one of you boys smoke these?'

'No.' We all three shook our heads. Katya herself never smokes. Erik and Specs and I smoke a pipe now and then, but not really very often, because we don't any of us particularly like the taste. To be perfectly honest, I think we really only smoke at all because it looks sort of sophisticated, and we rarely smoke cigarettes. I picked up the empty packet and examined it. It was wet, of course, but apart from that it looked fairly new. It couldn't have been lying here more than four or five days, at the most. And it was five days ago we'd buried the treasure.

'We can be pretty well sure it was the thief who threw that packet away,' said Specs. 'It would be a funny coincidence if there was anyone else here at the time. No, it must have been him!'

'I agree,' I said. 'It's a clue all right, only unfortunately it doesn't tell us much. Several million people must smoke this brand of cigarette.'

'We can start from here, though, and see where we get to,' Erik suggested.

I smoothed out the packet and put it in the driest of my pockets. Not that I thought it was a very promising clue, but it was the only one we had for the time being.

'We'd better make tracks for home now. Let's hope no one's discovered we're out.'

We trudged home through the wet wood. We were drenched ourselves, and extremely dismal. We had felt so rich, we were looking forward so much to giving Specs a surprise! And now . . .

We hardly said a word. I suppose we were all too busy thinking it over from every possible angle, trying to find something that would give us a pointer to the thief, so that we could get on his trail and catch him. We crossed the park and came out on the main road. There we all stopped suddenly. In the east the sky was a glaring red, from the flames of an enormous fire blazing away under the low, heavy clouds. Even from where we were, you could smell the smoke.

'That's High Farm burning!'

'Shall we run over and see?'

We stood there for a moment, undecided. It was really high time we went home; it was very late by now.

'Oh, come on – it'll only take a minute. Let's go and have a look.'

It isn't very often there's a fire at one of the big farms hereabouts, and I'm sure you will agree that we really couldn't turn our backs on it without a single look. So we set off at a trot across the wet fields. I was wondering how I was going to get my clothes dry enough for my aunt and uncle not to notice anything. I didn't want them finding out about this nocturnal expedition of ours.

Specs shouted breathlessly, 'The lightning must have struck it – set it on fire! Good grief, look at those flames!'

As we got closer we could see it was only the barn burning. The barn is some way from the actual farm, and luckily the wind was blowing away from the farmhouse and the other buildings, so they were not in danger. We knew that barn quite well; we used to play in it sometimes. It was quite easy to slip inside without being seen by anyone in the house. We'd been discovered once or twice, but we'd got off with a word of warning from the farmer, nothing worse. We liked the farmer. He was a good sort, easy-going, and we felt that it was a shame the lightning had to go and strike his farm.

We saw the dark shapes of a group of people outlined against the flames. The fire brigade from Hilleröd were there and the firemen were pumping water on the roofs of the still intact farm buildings. It looked as if they'd given up the barn itself as a bad job. We went quite close to the blaze, but then had to retreat. There's something fascinating about a fire like that on a dark night, and we stood there in silence, staring at the flames.

But suddenly we remembered the time. This was really it – we absolutely had to get home as fast as we could now. We ran back across the fields at top speed, and parted at the crossroads. Specs and Katya went off together in one direction, and Erik and I went in the other direction, which was our quickest way home.

'What a night!' gasped Erik.

'How right you are! If only I had some idea how to find the thief! Erik, could you go to the wood with Specs tomorrow and look for clues – help him with the fingerprints and so on?'

'Sure. What are you planning to do yourself?'

'I'll nip into Hilleröd and find out the

numbers of the bank-notes. I've just thought of that. They were all brand new.'

'Good idea,' Erik agreed.

We ran past the dingy pink villa where Laursen lives. In summer Laursen works as a kind of beach attendant, and we weren't specially fond of him. There was something about his face that reminded you of a rat. He was always in a bad temper, and forever picking on us for something or other. As we ran past his house I cast a quick glance at the windows, and I saw Laursen sitting there with his nose pressed to the glass, watching us.

'Kim,' said Erik, 'we've just *got* to get those thousand *kroner* back!'

'Dead right. I wish I knew how, that's all.'

'Maybe we'll think of something tomorrow.'

We ran the whole way home, splashing through puddles and over muddy patches. Our shoes were so wet anyway they couldn't very well get any wetter.

As I ran, I gasped, 'Did you see Laursen? He was sitting at his window watching us.'

'Well, what about it? Who cares for Laursen?'

I was home now. I whispered, 'Good night!' to Erik, and crept up to my room. I'd left the kitchen door open, so I managed to get into the house all right without making any noise. I hung my wet clothes over the back of a chair to dry and hurried into bed.

It was already beginning to get light. I lay awake for a bit, going over the whole story in my mind. But it was a funny thing, I kept thinking of Laursen's face. I didn't like the fact that he had seen us, though I couldn't quite say why.

Oh, don't be a fool, I told myself. It doesn't mean a thing.

But the very next day I was to find out how wrong I was!

Chapter 3

'Breakfast's ready, Kim!'

I woke with a start, and for a moment I couldn't remember where I was. I thought I was in bed at home in Copenhagen, and I had to get up and go to school. Then I realized it was the holidays, and the bed where I was lying was in my uncle's house on the north coast of Zealand, and I was spending the summer there, so it was my aunt outside the door calling me down for breakfast.

'Thanks, Aunt Olga. I'll be down in a minute.'

But I stayed in bed a little longer, listening to her footsteps as she went downstairs. It was a beautiful morning. The sun was shining, and it was quite warm in my room, which is right under the roof, but I could tell that the air was a lot cooler after last night's storm. So I lay there, thinking things over – all the things that had happened to me since I crept out of the house yesterday evening. For a split second I'd hoped it was just a dream, but then I caught sight of the clothes hung over the chair to dry, and I knew I couldn't have dreamt that. So the thousand *kroner* really *had* been stolen! Then I remembered about the fire, and running home, and once again Laursen's face suddenly flashed in front of my eyes. I saw him watching Erik and me through the window, and I just hoped he wouldn't go telling tales to my uncle. It must be my guilty conscience that made Laursen keep coming into my mind. Well, I suppose I shouldn't really have left the house at night without asking my uncle and aunt's permission. They'd have been sure to give it; it was just that they always liked to know where I was going, which I suppose was reasonable enough, come to think of it. I got dressed and had a wash (or rather, the other way round) and went downstairs. I was glad they hadn't noticed anything. I knew that already; I could tell from my aunt's voice when she called me down to breakfast.

My uncle looked up from his coffee cup as I came in.

'Morning, Kim! Heard about the fire at High Farm last night?'

'A fire?'

'Caused by lightning, apparently. They say the place has been burnt to the ground. A shocking thing – the poor farmer!'

I nodded. I couldn't very well correct him and tell him that only the barn had burned down. I was glad to see him bury himself in his paper. I could feel my face going red! There are some times when you have to tell a lie, but I'm not very good at it. I got down to my breakfast, letting my mind wander to the problem of our missing treasure now and again.

Last night, I'd decided to go to Hilleröd and ask the bank to tell me the numbers of my lost hundred *kroner* notes, but since then it had occurred to me that I could find out just as easily over the phone. I was sure the cashier would remember me; we'd had quite a long talk when I drew out the money.

Before I go on, I'd better tell you something about this money, because of course if you haven't read about us before, you won't know how we came to have so much cash.

Well, I got the money from a publishing firm in Copenhagen for writing a book called *Kim the Detective*, and in this book I wrote about the first part of our holidays here on the north coast of Zealand, and some people think it's quite a good story. I'm not so sure myself; the thing is that when I wrote it I didn't intend it to be a real book. I just wanted to put the things that happened to us down on paper, because they suddenly seemed to be getting so exciting that I felt I had to record them. However, it turned out to be a book after all; you can find out how that happened from the end of *Kim the Detective*, if you feel like reading it.

So in fact the thousand *kroner* were really mine, but I didn't see it that way, because though I had done the actual writing of the story, and put it in my own words, it was the others who had got the whole thing going, and Specs in particular. And so when I was wondering what to do with the money, I had the idea of giving it to Specs. Or rather, using it for his invention. I didn't mind exactly how he used it in detail. He'd need some of the money for the old car he and Stoffer wanted to use for trying out his new carburettor, and as for any that was left over, as far as I was concerned he could give it to his parents, or save it for his studies, or anything else he liked. Anyway, I wanted it to be *his* money, and I hoped he wouldn't be too proud to accept it.

I told the others my plan, and they were all for it. So I persuaded the publisher to make the cheque out to me and not my father, which was what he wanted to do at first. But I told him why, and he thought it was a good idea. He knew about Specs from my book, and he promised not to mention the money to my parents until I'd told them about it myself. He kept his promise, too. But then he came to see my uncle one day, and he did tell him. (They were sitting down in the summerhouse, and I could hear them from up in my room.) And my uncle told my father – or at least, he wrote him a letter, so now my parents know after all. The funny thing is that they didn't know *I* know *they* know. They never mentioned it when they wrote, and I didn't mention it when I wrote back.'

Anyway, it was this money that had been stolen. I sat for quite a time trying to pluck up courage to ring the bank. You wouldn't think a simple telephone call would take that much courage, but that's the way I am when I know everything is up to me. I feel very respectful towards banks and so on – well, naturally I've never had much to do with that sort of place. A bank is an important, serious place. Going into a bank and drawing out a thousand *kroner* is different from going to the chemist's and buying a bar of soap. I mean, you do need more courage! The people behind the counters are all very correctly dressed, even on hot summer days. They're reserved, and rather solemn. Still, they're nice, all the same. But a boy in jeans, with untidy hair, in a bank is like a dog in church. This was why I sat for quite a time wondering, just what to say over the phone.

It made me feel as if our hunt for the stolen money was only an exciting game, and even when I forced myself to remember that it was serious enough in all conscience, I still couldn't get rid of this feeling that it was all a game, which made everything rather difficult. You don't go dragging banks into your games!

But finally, when my aunt was out in the kitchen, I pulled myself together and made my call. I asked to speak to the cashier and told him who I was.

'Oh, yes, I remember you!' he said. 'You're the young man who cashed a cheque for a thousand *kroner* last week, aren't you?'

'Yes, that's right. And I . . . er . . . I wanted to know if you'd be kind enough to tell me the numbers of the notes. They were all new.'

'Why do you say "they were"?'

'What?' I asked, playing for time.

'I said, why did you say "they were"? Haven't you got them any more?'

'Oh, yes – yes, of course I have!' I replied. 'I mean, no! I mean, it's a long story! It's just that I'd like to know the numbers. But perhaps you can't tell me?'

'Well, I must say, I don't quite get *your* number!' said the cashier, laughing. 'Why do you want the numbers? Now, listen, young man, if you've lost the money, you must go straight to the . . .'

'No, no, I haven't lost it! I've got it here!'

'Did you say you've got it there? Then why ring up and ask for the numbers? You can read them for yourself!'

'Well . . . well, I don't actually have it right here in front of me, not at this very moment.'

I could feel my face going redder than ever. I wished I'd never had this mindless notion of ringing up the bank!

'Hmph!' said the cashier. 'There's something funny about this, if you ask me Still, I can certainly tell you the numbers. Just wait a moment while I look them up. It was Wednesday you were in here, wasn't it?'

'Yes, that's right. And thanks – thanks very much.'

He went away, and came back to the phone soon afterwards to tell me the numbers. I wrote them down on a piece of paper and thanked him profusely.

Well, I thought, that's that. Phew, that

was tricky! But now we had two clues to follow up: the empty cigarette packet and the numbers of the notes. Not that either clue seemed exactly promising . . .

I had got this far in my thoughts when my aunt came into the room.

'Kim, could you run down to the shop for me?'

'Yes, of course, Aunt Olga.'

'I just want half a kilo of icing sugar, six eggs, two kilos of potatoes, two tomatoes, quarter of a kilo of coffee, a tin of fishballs, and a dishcloth.'

I thought: did she say *just*?

'Can you remember all that?' she asked.

'Of course!' I said, grandly.

'Tell me what it was, then!'

'Er, well, a dishcloth, and . . . er . . . four eggs and . . .'

'Six eggs, I said!'

'That's right, six. And . . . um . . . a tin of fishballs, right?'

'Oh, do listen!' said my aunt crossly. 'Pull yourself together, Kim! I said: half a kilo of icing sugar, a dishcloth, a tin of fishballs, two tomatoes, six eggs, two kilos of potatoes and a quarter of a kilo of coffee. That's not difficult to remember, is it? Seven items in all.'

She gave me the money, and I set off. She stood in the doorway, waving, as if I were a little boy going shopping on my own for the first time. I like my aunt, but sometimes she forgets I'll be fifteen in a few months' time. Since there was no one around to see me, I turned and waved back.

It was going to be a real midsummer's day. The sun was burning down, the heat beat up from the asphalt, and the road was full of holiday-makers in swimsuits. The thought of a swim was tempting. If it hadn't been for our missing money, I'd have been in a very good mood. But I couldn't stop thinking about the lost treasure, and at the same time I kept repeating: 'A dishcloth, a tin of fishballs, two tomatoes, half a kilo of icing sugar, two kilos of potatoes, six eggs, a quarter of a kilo of coffee. Seven items in all.'

I don't exactly recall the details, but somehow or other I suddenly found myself standing outside Katya's garden gate, which was rather surprising, because if I was going to the shop this was right out of my way. Still, I thought that if, quite by chance, I'd ended up here I might as well wait around and see if Katya came out. So I sat down outside the gate on a white-painted stone.

I waited for a good fifteen minutes, but finally, as Katya did not put in an appearance, I got up again and went back the same way I'd come. How did it go? A dishcloth, seven eggs, a tin of fishballs, quarter of a kilo of coffee, two kilos of potatoes, a tomato, a kilo of icing sugar, six items in all. Yes, that was it! Perhaps Katya had gone to do some shopping too, in which case I'd meet her down at the shop, and we could go back together. I thought I might suggest a swim later.

A dishcloth.
A tin of fishballs.
Seven kilos of potatoes.
Two eggs, one tomato.
Quarter of a kilo of icing sugar.
Six items in all.

When I got to the shop I found the place full, and I had a good look round as I waited. Our local shop is a genuine, old-fashioned general store, with ropes and nets and all kinds of sailing and fishing equipment hanging on the walls, and it smells of tar and spices and tobacco. There are so many things to see that you could never be bored here.

Other customers were coming in behind me. Suddenly I heard a laugh – a laugh that I knew. The man from the wood! Someone had made a joke which I didn't catch, and several people laughed, among them the man from the wood.

I turned round to take a look at him. He was poorly dressed, almost like a tramp, and his chin was covered with stubble. The stubble was nearly white; he was older than I'd thought last night. His clothes were very shabby, just rags, really, but his face was nicer than I'd expected.

'What can I do for you?'

'Er . . . what?' I stammered.

'You're next. What do you want?'

'Oh . . . er . . . a tomato.'

'One tomato. Anything else?'

'No, that's all. Oh yes – three kilos of granulated sugar!'

The shopkeeper went off to weigh out the sugar. 'Your auntie beginning on her ham-making already, is she?' he asked as he brought it over, with a friendly smile.

'Yes . . . I mean, I think so,' I said absent-mindedly. Then I remembered something else. 'Oh, and she wants a dishcloth too.'

The tramp was being served by a shop assistant now. I was afraid he might be finished before me, and disappear. He bought a box of matches, a bar of chocolate, and a packet of cigarettes – ten Kings.

Not Broadways, Kings. This was a bit of a disappointment to me, but it probably didn't mean much. After all, who said he always had to smoke the same brand?

'Anything else?'

'A tin of fishballs.'

The shopkeeper climbed a ladder and got the tin down from a shelf. His movements struck me as particularly slow today.

'And a kilo of potatoes!' I added. 'Four items in all.'

He fetched the potatoes, and corrected me. 'No, five!'

'It comes to the same thing. Oh, do be quick!'

He stared at me curiously as I paid. The tramp had already left the shop.

Chapter 4

The tramp was going towards the wood, which as far as I was concerned was the wrong way, since my aunt was waiting at home for her shopping. But I felt this was more important, and I was sure she'd forgive me if she knew how much money was at stake. So I went the other way, following the tramp. He seemed to have plenty of time to spare. He looked in all the shop windows, standing in front of some of them for quite a time, but he never turned round.

Then I ran straight into Specs.

'Hullo,' he said. 'This is a bit of luck, meeting you. I need your finger-prints. Eric and I went out to the hut, and we found no end of finger-prints, only we don't know whose they are. But . . .'

I grabbed his arm to interrupt him.

'Never mind the finger-prints!' I whispered urgently. 'That's the thief – that man over there!'

'Wh-what? Who? Him? Over there? How do you know?'

'I recognized his laugh. That's the man I heard following me in the wood last night.'

'Are you sure?'

'Positive. Listen, Specs, could you take these things home to my aunt, while I follow him? I've got to shadow him – only Aunt Olga's waiting for the shopping.'

'No,' said Specs, tersely. '*I'll* shadow him, *you* take your aunt's shopping home, and after that you go off to my lab and have Erik take your finger-prints! Go on, be sensible! After all, why shouldn't I do the shadowing? I've got time, and what do you suppose I'd tell your aunt? There you are, see! You go home and leave him to me. Anyway, he may have seen you at the shop, but he won't know me, that's for sure.'

Specs stuck to his guns, and finally I gave in. We fixed it that he'd return to the rest of us in an hour's time and report, and if we weren't in the garage (Specs's lab, that is) he'd find us on the beach.

I picked the shopping bag up again and started for home. I turned once, and saw the man from the wood, a long way off, with Specs following him at a distance, stalking him like an Indian.

When I got home, my aunt was rather surprised by the results of my shopping. She said I'd brought all the wrong things and the wrong quantities, so I had to go back to the shop, but this time she wrote me out a list. As I left the house, she called after me, Kim!'

'Yes?'

'The seat of your trousers is all white.'

'I must have been sitting on a white stone,' I said, casually.

'Oh, Kim, you're a hopeless case!' said my aunt, sighing. But I could tell from her voice that she wasn't really cross with me any more.

So I went back to the shop, and this time I bought the right things. I kept an eye open for Katya again, but I still didn't see her. I kept wondering how Specs was getting on, shadowing the tramp, and I felt rather annoyed that it wasn't me following him, because I consider myself a bit of an expert at shadowing people.

When I got home again, Aunt Olga said, 'Oh, Erik was here looking for you. He asked me to tell you they want you over in Specs's lab – he said it was very important.'

'Thanks, I'll go over at once. Er . . . so long as you don't want me here? Can I do anything to help?' I asked politely.

My aunt laughed and shook her head.

'No thanks! Kim – you're not up to anything silly in that laboratory, are you?'

'No, of course we aren't! What made you think that?' I said soothingly.

'Well, I don't like it . . . playing around with all those chemicals, and the rest of the stuff you have there. One of these days you'll be blowing yourselves sky-high.'

'No, honestly, we're very careful,' I told her. 'Specs understands all about it, and he's in charge. We aren't making any gunpowder today, I promise!'

'Well, mind you're back for lunch.'

'You bet!'

'And do be careful crossing the road. Such a lot of traffic . . .'

'Yes, Aunt Olga.'

'And Kim!'

'Yes, Aunt Olga?'

'The seat of your trousers is *still* all white!'

I finally managed to get away, and seconds later I was flinging my bike to the ground outside Specs's lab. The door was open, and Erik was standing inside the lab, bending over some pieces of paper. He looked up as I came in.

'Hi,' he said. 'Come over here and let me take your finger-prints, Kim.'

'Sure,' I said. 'How do you do it?'

'You'll see.' He took my wrist, and pressed the tips of my fingers down on an inkpad. 'Right, now all you have to do is put your fingers here, on this piece of paper. Then we've got you nailed! Well, we've got you nailed anyway, only we want to be quite sure which finger-prints are whose! Look, these must be yours.'

He produced a piece of paper bearing a finger-print about the size of a saucer.

'Oh, come off it!' I grinned. 'I've never had fingers that large!'

'How dim can you get?' groaned Erik in mock horror. 'Listen will, you? Specs and I went off to the wood first thing this morning, taking with us, of course, the finger-print powder always carried by any self-respecting detective for such emergencies! Out in the hut we dusted all the smooth surfaces with it. That shows up the finger-prints, see? We found everyone's prints on the tin that held the money – we'd all been handling it: you and me and Katya and Specs.

'These little prints here must be Katya's; she's got the smallest fingers. Now I'll show you the thief's prints. I've made sketches of all five sorts of prints we found, and there's one set of prints which doesn't belong to any of us. Look at that print you've just made on the paper! Right – now take a good look at these two sketches – those other three belong to Specs and Katya and me. Now then, which is yours?'

'That one,' I said at once.

'Write "Kim" over it,' he told me. Then he took the pencil and wrote 'The Thief' above the other sketch.

I was much impressed. It was a brilliant idea to make enlarged copies of all the prints; the lines showed up much more clearly, and even though the sketches might not be perfect in every tiny detail, they were close enough to show up the differences between the five finger-prints quite distinctly.

I told Erik about my telephone conversation with the bank.

'This is great!' he cried. 'The net is closing in around him! We didn't have a single clue to start with, and now we've got three: the cigarette packet, the numbers of the bank-notes, and the finger-prints. If we keep on at this rate we'll have him in no time.'

'Well, we'll have him any minute now, actually!' I said, making it sound casual. 'Specs will be back in a few moments, and he'll be able to tell us where the thief lives!'

'Wh-what?' stammered Erik, staring at me. 'What on earth do you mean? What *is* all this?'

So I told him how I'd met the thief, and Specs was shadowing him.

'Good grief, why didn't you say so before?'

'I didn't want you chasing off after them too. Better leave it to Specs. If we go as well we might ruin it all.'

'You may have a point there . . . but you know, I think it's funny, him buying packets of ten cigarettes! I mean, now that he's got a thousand *kroner*! He's got plenty of money to buy a big packet. Oh, well, there may be a reason for it! You know, this is getting really exciting! But I'll have to go home for lunch now,' Erik remembered. 'Tell you what – let's meet down on the beach after lunch. I'll drop in at Katya's on my way home and tell her. Specs will know where to look for us when he comes back.'

I went home to lunch too, and after lunch I went up to my room for my swimming things. I thought it was rather odd that we still hadn't heard anything from Specs. Well, perhaps he was at home having lunch; I knew they didn't have very regular mealtimes in his family, but of course I was longing to hear what he'd been doing. Then I heard my uncle's voice downstairs.

'He's just gone up to his room,' he was saying. 'Yes, you can go up – that's right, up the stairs there.'

I hoped it was Specs, but then I heard quick, light footsteps on the stairs: Katya's footsteps. She knocked and came in.

'Hullo, Kim!' she said cheerfully. 'I just thought I'd see if you were coming swimming.'

Then, closing the door behind her, she whispered, 'You'd better get out, quick! The police have just been over and taken Erik away! Laursen told them he'd seen you two last night, and they think you set fire to the barn!'

Chapter 5

I just stood there, my mind a blank.

'Kim, you must get out of here! Don't you see – they'll be arriving any minute now!'

Well, I certainly would have liked to take Katya's advice and get out! On the other hand, could I leave Erik in the lurch? After all, we *hadn't* started the fire. Innocent as a couple of newborn babes, that was us. I realized we'd have to drag Specs into this. He could prove we were in the wood with him at the moment that the fire broke out. Still, what a mess!

'Quick, Kim, *hurry*!'

I shook my head. 'No, there wouldn't be any point in it, Katya. Thanks for coming to warn me, though. Listen: if Erik hasn't said anything about you being there at the hut with us, I'll keep my mouth shut too. There's no reason for you to be involved. We'll just tell them we and Specs were at the hut in the wood, and then we'll get Specs along and ask him if that's right, and he'll prove it is, and then they'll let us go. There's nothing to worry about.'

'Are you sure?'

'Positive. Look, will you run over to see Specs and give him the word – tell him not to mention you if they come to fetch him!'

She nodded. 'I don't like it, though,' she murmured, 'I'd much rather you cleared out.'

'But that would really give them a reason to think we'd done something wrong, Katya. And anyway, where would I...'

I didn't finish my sentence, because voices came drifting up from downstairs. I heard my uncle say, 'Oh, come, this is ridiculous! Yes, I'd take my oath he was at home all last night. However, we can ask the boy himself, if you like. Kim!'

I opened the door. 'Yes?' I called.

'It's the police; they want a word with you. Come right down, will you?'

'Goodbye, Kim.'

Katya gave me her hand, and I pressed it, with a funny kind of glow inside me. She was taking it all so seriously! Just as if I was being carted off to the scaffold or something!

'Remember, you wait up here till they've taken me away, and then run off and tell Specs,' I whispered. 'He must be back by now. So long!'

She looked as if she was about to burst into tears any moment, so I hastily shut the door behind me and ran downstairs. My uncle was standing in the hall, looking very serious. There was a uniformed policeman with him. Quite a young one, not our local policeman Larsen – he was probably from Hilleröd.

I said how do you do politely.

'The Inspector here says you were seen near High Farm last night. Is that so, Kim?'

'Er . . . yes, Uncle Carlo.'

'You mean you went out without telling me or your aunt, and you were wandering around the place without our permission?'

'Well . . . yes. Yes, I'm sorry,' I said in a subdued voice. Then I raised my head. He wasn't looking so angry as I'd expected.

'And what were you up to at the farm?' asked the policeman.

'We went to have a look at the fire.'

'Who's "we"?'

'Erik and Specs and me.'

My uncle interrupted. 'Look here, Kim, if you really *were* in the barn smoking, or anything like that, it'd be better to admit it now,' he said seriously. 'The police will find out anyway.'

'Yes, I know, but we *weren't* in the barn. We were only in the wood . . .'

'In the wood? What were you up to in the wood?' asked the policeman.

'We've got a hut there,' I explained. 'And when we were coming home we saw the fire out at the farm, so we ran over to have a look. We thought it must have been struck by lightning.'

'Mm. Well, I'm afraid I must ask you to come with me in any case, just to answer a few questions. You'll be seeing him back quite soon, Mr Nörmark, if he has nothing to do with the fire. We're only going to the police station here; his friend's there already. Let's hope they're both telling the truth and can prove it!'

'I'm sure they are!' said my uncle quietly. 'Well, goodbye for now, Kim.'

'Goodbye, Uncle. And – look, I'm sorry I didn't ask permission to go out!'

'All right, all right! Off you go, now!' He gave me a pat on the shoulder and pushed me gently out of the door.

It took us only a few minutes to drive to the police station, where Larsen, our local policeman, lived. It was on the main road, just outside the village. The little office of the police station was crammed with people: Larsen himself, and Laursen who'd seen us last night, a uniformed policeman from the town, and a man in plain clothes, whom I didn't know. Erik was sitting on the sofa. When I came in we nodded to each other, and he winked at me. I wondered what he was trying to convey to me; probably he meant I wasn't to mention Katya. Larsen (who is very nice, by the way) asked me to give my version of what had happened. So I did, and I got the impression that he believed me. (I didn't say anything about the buried treasure. I felt sure Erik wouldn't have mentioned that either.) But then Laursen put his oar in.

'Well, anyone can see these two young scoundrels have made that story up between them! *I* saw them wink at each other when this lad here was brought in. *And* I saw the way they came running away from High Farm when it was burning. It's not the first time they've been found hanging around that barn. You can bet they were in there, smoking, and now they're trying to wriggle out of it!'

'Do you smoke?' the man in plain clothes asked me.

'No,' I said.

'That's a lie!' cried Laursen. 'That's a downright, wicked lie! I saw them with my own eyes, down on the beach. That one –' and he pointed to me – 'that one has a corn-cob pipe, and the pair of them both smoke it!'

'Is that true, Kim?' asked Larsen.

'Well, yes.'

'Then why did you lie to us just now, boy? Do your parents let you smoke?'

'Well, we're allowed to smoke a bit,' I explained. 'But only pipes, just now and then.'

'Humph! I don't know what young people are coming to. If you were my boys I wouldn't allow any such thing! However ... you will stick to it that you weren't at the farm – you didn't get there until the barn was already burning?'

'That's right,' Erik and I replied in chorus.

'And you also say you were out at your hut in the wood with a boy called Specs? His real name is Palle, isn't it? They're staying in the brown bungalow over there, him and his parents, right?'

'Yes.'

'Well, then, we'll send over for him and hear what his story is, but personally I think you two are telling the truth. Laursen, did you know about this hut of theirs in the wood?'

Laursen shook his head. 'Oh, I never go right in there! You don't mean to say you're letting this precious pair go?'

'We'll just see what young Specs has to say,' Larsen told him. 'And the police investigating the fire, too. They'll most likely find out what really caused it within the day.'

A policeman had already gone off to fetch Specs. We waited. No one in the little room spoke. The clock on the wall was ticking; I thought I'd never heard a clock tick so loud before. Erik's head was bent, and he was staring at the toes of his shoes. I wondered what Specs had been doing all this time. What had he found out about the man from the wood? What news would he have for us when the police had let us go? We heard the car come back, and the policeman came into the room.

'Not at home. His parents say he didn't come home to lunch, and they don't know where he is, so I couldn't bring him in.'

'This is ridiculous,' said Larsen, irritated. 'Now what?'

'Well, I told his parents to send him along as soon as he does come home.'

'Good. Well, that's about it for the time being, eh? Do you think we can let these lads go?'

'I don't see why not,' decided the plain-clothes policeman. 'We'll see what the fire investigators have to say before we make any more inquiries. Off you run, you two!'

We didn't wait to be told twice. But we were hardly out of the door when Larsen called us back.

'Just one thing! You say you have a hut in the wood . . . it's not you setting snares out there, is it?'

'Snares?' I asked, taken aback.

'That's right. Traps to catch animals.'

'No, it's not us.'

'I'm glad to hear that, I must say . . . tormenting poor dumb creatures! I'd like to get my hands on whoever *is* behind it. You say it's not you?'

'Definitely not!'

'We wouldn't do a thing like that,' Erik assured Larsen.

'All right, all right! I didn't really think you would. Off you go, then.'

And we found ourselves outside the door again. After the dim light in Larsen's office the sun was dazzlingly bright.

'What do you think Specs is up to?' Erik wondered. 'Do you think anything's happened to him?'

'No idea. He ought to have been back long before this.'

We stood around for a bit, not sure what

to do next. We didn't even know which way to go in order to look for Specs. Maybe the tramp had seen Specs shadowing him and knocked him unconscious. Maybe he was in some other kind of danger. But we had no notion *where* to find him; all we did know was that he had followed the man towards the wood.

'Don't you think we'd better get home now?' said Erik. 'They'll be expecting us. Then we can get away again, as quickly as possible, and start looking for Specs.'

'Right – let's meet in fifteen minutes' time at the lab,' I said.

'OK,' he agreed. 'I just hope I can manage to get away without too much fuss, that's all! I'll do my best.'

We had already parted when I thought of something else, so I called after Erik and ran back.

'I've just thought – why don't you bring Schnapp along?'

'OK, boss,' said Erik. 'Er . . . what for?'

'Well, he might come in useful in all

sorts of ways,' I said. 'He might even get on Specs's scent for us.'

'He *might* . . . provided Specs happened to be standing ten metres away from him waving a large sausage in the air. Otherwise, I wouldn't count on it. Still, we can always try! Fifteen minutes?'

'Fifteen minutes.'

Chapter 6

I borrowed my uncle's bike, which was the first that came to hand, and shot across to the lab. The door was open, and when I went in I found Erik there already, sitting on the floor trying to persuade Schnapp to sniff Specs's white overall. Schnapp was not at all keen. In fact, he was vigorously resisting Erik's persuasions.

I grinned, and Erik looked up, with an injured expression. 'All right then, *you* try if you think you can do any better,' he said.

Grabbing Schnapp's nose, he forced it down to the overall. Schnapp broke away and dashed out of the garage, and we heard him sneezing outside. I picked up the overall and had a sniff myself, and I found I was sneezing too.

'Perhaps it smells of something that made Schnapp sneeze,' said Erik, looking as if he'd just invented gunpowder or made some such world-shaking discovery.

'A brilliant piece of deduction,' I said sarcastically. 'A right little Sherlock Holmes, aren't you! *You* smell it, then!'

I threw the overall at him.

'It's those wretched chemicals, and all that stuff he mucks about with!' said Erik crossly. 'I must say, I don't blame Schnapp – *I* wouldn't want to smell the stuff. But what are we supposed to do? This is the only one of Specs's clothes I can find. I daren't go and ask his mother for something else; she'd be bound to ask why we wanted it.'

'No, that wouldn't be any good. Well, we'll just have to do without Schnapp and try to get on the trail ourselves somehow or other.'

Closing the garage door behind us, we cycled off to the wood, and shortly afterwards Schnapp came galloping up behind us. Apparently he'd decided to join the hunt after all. We rode to the beginning of the path where we'd heard the man last night, left our bikes there, and went into the wood on foot.

We were walking quite fast, but all the same we didn't forget to have a good look all round us as we walked. Schnapp ran about and got underfoot, and thought it was all a marvellous game.

As we were walking along the path, I thought about everything that had happened since I was here last night. In fact, so much had happened that it was quite confusing; I didn't know just where to find the end of string that would unravel the knot if I pulled it. But perhaps we'd find the solution staring us in the face once we'd tracked down Specs.

Once we'd tracked down Specs! The phrase sounded so vague, as if we might *not* track him down, that I didn't like it at all. I pictured all sorts of awful things that might account for our failure to find him. Scenes from creepy films appeared before my mind's eye, while all the crime stories

I'd ever read flashed through my mind. Suppose . . . suppose someone had murdered Specs! Suppose we found him here in the middle of the wood, cold and dead! I'd never forgive myself for agreeing to let him follow the thief instead of me. I ought to have gone myself . . . but then *I* might be lying somewhere in the wood, cold and dead, horribly murdered!

How were we ever going to explain it to his parents?

'Kim,' said Erik gloomily. 'You know, if anything's happened to Specs, I bet we never get permission to go to the hut again!'

We both quickened our pace. We had no real idea where to look, but we felt as though it would help matters if only we walked *fast*. That at least gave us the feeling that we were doing something!

I couldn't get Specs out of my mind, so I was glad to have my thoughts interrupted by Erik beginning to talk about the buried treasure.

And while we were half running, half walking along like this, talking to each other in low voices, I had, for the first time, an odd feeling that I'd already solved the mystery! I seemed to have the answer somewhere inside my head, but I just couldn't quite pin it down. It was as if I'd discovered something in the course of the day which told me quite clearly who the thief was. I didn't mention it to Erik, who would simply have thought I was right off my head. I tried to remember, mentally running through all the things I'd done since I got up in the morning. It was no good, I couldn't lay my hand on it.

'And listen, Kim,' Erik said, going off on another tack, 'I don't think that old cigarette packet is much of a clue, really. When I think of the crowds of people who smoke Broadways . . . well, I mean, even one of those policemen, does, and Laursen, and Larsen himself!'

'Oh, sure, it must have been them!' I muttered between my teeth. 'That's right,

Larsen's our man! No, seriously, of course I noticed that too. And the other policeman smokes North State; I saw the cigarette packet in his pocket. No, you're right. The empty cigarette packet doesn't mean a thing.'

Suddenly Erik grabbed my arm.

'There's someone coming! Quick! Into the bushes!'

We crawled into the undergrowth and tried to hold our breath. Erik was lying half on top of Schnapp, holding his jaws clamped together. The dog was struggling and clawing to get free, but Erik was stronger. The footsteps were coming closer, fast. They came from behind us, the same way we had come. My arm was lying on a prickly twig, but I didn't dare take it away in case I made a noise.

The steps stopped just by our hiding place. Cautiously, I lifted my head and peered through the brushwood. Then I jumped up and was out on the path in a couple of strides. It was only Katya!

'Hullo,' she said. 'What are you two doing, crawling around the bushes?'

'We didn't know it was you,' I said, not too logically.

'That's no reason to hide,' she said, sure enough. 'Anyway, what are you doing here in the wood?'

I realized that Katya, of course, knew nothing about the mysterious disappearance of Specs. I told her the story, as briefly as possible, and she looked horrified.

'That's it, so you'd better go home straight away,' Erik told her. 'We'll come over to your place as soon as we get back and tell you what happened.'

'Why can't I come with you?'

'Oh, for goodness' sake!' said Erik impatiently. 'This is no time to have girls around...'

'Nonsense!' she interrupted sharply. Erik shrugged his shoulders, and shut up.

'How did you find us?' I asked, as we all three walked on along the path. 'Of course – you must have seen us making for the wood. But how did you know we'd gone along this particular path? Did you hear us?'

She stared at me for a moment, apparently nonplussed. 'Oh, *Kim*!' she said. 'Why do you *always* think I must be stupid? Naturally, I followed the signs you left behind you! I've got eyes in my head!'

Erik and I stopped dead. 'What signs?'

'The bent twigs,' she said. 'Why – did you leave any other signs too?'

'What bent twigs?' asked Erik. 'Listen, Katya, if there are any bent twigs around here, *we* didn't leave them!'

'But perhaps Specs did!' I said.

Katya began to look as if she were just a little less cross with us. Then she took us back along the path and showed us one of these signs. It was clear enough: a small twig, half snapped off and bent to point the way we were going. Neither Erik nor I had noticed the twigs marking our route, and we both felt pretty silly.

'Well, if you didn't leave the signs, how do *you* come to be going the right way?' Katya asked.

'Oh, shut up, do!' muttered Erik.

We went on; we kept finding more of the bent twigs, and we followed them till they led us to another path, along which we walked for some time. It took us deeper and deeper into the wood.

Suddenly Schnapp leaped forward and dashed off. Erik called him back in a hoarse whisper, but Schnapp took no notice. He tore across a clearing and through some bushes on the other side. We heard him bark, but it didn't sound angry, more of an excited, happy bark. We followed him across the clearing, and through the bushes. And there was Specs, sitting beside our 'man from the wood'!

Schnapp ran all round us in circles, panting happily, enormously pleased with himself for finding Specs.

Specs stood up.

'Hi!' he said. 'How did you get here –

did you see the signs I left to mark the way?'

'Katya did,' admitted Erik, briefly.

Specs grinned, and introduced us, with an impressive wave of his hand. The Man from the Wood nodded, and invited us to sit down, which we did. Seen at close quarters, our tramp looked a bit the worse for wear, but quite friendly and nice really.

'Well, I'd better tell you all about it!' Specs said. 'But before I start I'd just like to explain that it was *not* Mr Svensen here who dug up our money, so we still haven't found the thief!'

'*Mr* Svensen, eh?' said the tramp, laughing. 'It's a good few years since anybody called me mister! Keep it up, lad! Makes a change!'

'Well,' Specs began, 'I followed Mr Svensen after Kim put me on his track. It turned into a longish walk, because he was going round all the farms and . . . er . . .'

'And begging,' the man finished the

sentence. 'Go on, son, that's what I was doing, beggin'! No reason why you should be ashamed to say it if I'm not!'

'Well, all right, then, he was going round all the farms begging,' Specs went on. 'And I was following him, and the whole time I was thinking it was a bit funny for someone who'd just dug up a thousand *kroner* to be going round begging. The longer I thought about it, the more I felt he couldn't be the real thief. Finally I followed him out here into the wood. I kept bending back twigs as I went along, so you could find me if you came after me. It turns out that Mr Svensen lives here in the wood.'

Specs pointed to some sacks lying under a kind of shelter made of branches and twigs tied together, thatched with leaves.

'I saw Mr Svensen go in here,' he went on, 'so I lay down to hide in the bushes and wait. He sat down and started reading an old newspaper. Well, I should think over an hour went by, and still nothing happened.'

'I don't read so good!' said Mr Svensen, with a rueful laugh.

'And suddenly I got fed up with waiting, so I stood up and said hullo! Then I began asking Mr Svensen a few questions, like did he know about our treasure, and who did he think could have dug it up? We've been sitting here talking for the last fifteen minutes or so, and I've already found out one piece of information that may come in useful.'

'Which of you lads was it I scared last night, by the way?' asked the tramp.

'Him!' said Specs, pointing to me.

'Hm, well, sorry, son!' said the tramp. 'You sounded so funny hooting away like that! Bless you, I wasn't following you, son! I was just on my way back to my little place here!'

'It was stupid of me,' I admitted, feeling very small. 'Silly to be scared of a thing like that!'

'And now, you listen to this!' Specs went on. 'It looks as if the person who stole our money was a poacher who's been setting snares here in the wood. At least, there *is* a poacher around, and it seems more than likely that he was the one who saw you lot bury the treasure.'

'Wait a moment!' I interrupted. 'Erik and I have just been talking to Laursen – you see, the police suspected us of setting fire to High Farm last night, but they let us go again – and do you know who told on us? Laursen!'

'The rat!' added Erik, grinding his teeth.

'And as we were going, Larsen mentioned someone who'd been setting snares here in the wood, and said how much he'd like to lay hands on him.'

'It would be good if we could catch him!' said Specs. 'Mr Svensen here has seen him.'

'That's right. Not far from that hut of yours,' Svensen told us. 'I've stumbled over those nasty traps of his once or twice, I have. Found a squirrel in one of them only the other day, with a broken leg, poor thing. It was pretty near starved to death when I found it; I had to kill it. I said to myself: if I get hold of the fellow that did this, I said, I'll teach him a lesson! And one night I followed him. Four or five days ago, that would have been. I saw him bending over some of his traps, but it was dark, and I couldn't see too well. Had to keep my distance, anyway. He had a torch, and the light fell on him once or twice. What was he wearing now . . .? Light jacket, black trousers – well, dark trousers, anyway. I reckon he'd be a bit shorter than me. I only saw him from the back, though, and then I went and trod on a twig, and he switched off his torch and ran for it. Right towards the middle of the wood, that's the way he ran, towards your hut. I know that hut of yours pretty well – I've had a look round, been in there once or twice! I borrowed a bit of your baccy too, but don't you worry, I'll pay it back one of these days. Well, anyway, he slipped through my fingers that time, so I came back here to get some sleep. But then I was woken a bit later by someone going past not far off. That'll have been you kids. I could hear it was a couple of boys and a girl.'

'So that would have been the night you buried the treasure,' said Specs. 'And now that we know the thief was near the hut the same night, it's safe to assume he saw it all from a hiding-place.'

'Well, so far, so good,' said Erik, lighting his pipe. 'That gives us a line to follow, at least. But I don't see that it gets us very far.'

He passed me the tobacco. I took it and began to fill my pipe – only a little, right at the bottom of the bowl, because it was a new pipe and I hadn't really run it in yet. I passed the tobacco on to Svensen, who filled his pipe and offered it to Specs, but Specs refused and handed the tobacco back to Erik. Erik, putting it in his pocket, said, 'I mean, we don't know enough to be able to find him. It's the same with our other clues – the cigarette packet, the finger-prints, the numbers of the notes. They may all be perfectly good clues, only they don't lead us anywhere.'

'Wait a *minute*, though!' I shouted.

'What's up?'

'Yoohooo!'

'Are you completely nuts?'

'No!' I said, more calmly. 'But I've solved the mystery! Now I know who the thief is!'

Chapter 7

Everyone stared at me in speechless astonishment for a moment or so. Specs was the first to recover.

'You *know*?' he said. 'You know for sure?'

'Of course!'

'Well, who is it, then?' asked Katya.

'Just wait a minute,' I said. 'You'll see in a moment, only I've got to lead up to it properly. You remember my corn-cob pipe?'

'Yes, of course. What about it?'

'Where have you seen me smoking it?'

'At the hut,' said Specs.

'That's right. And where else?'

All three looked at me inquiringly. Svensen sat there in silence, watching us with a slight smile. His eyebrows were raised; he seemed to be thinking hard.

'Well, I've never seen you smoking it anywhere else,' said Erik. 'At least, not that I remember. But what's that got to do with all this?'

'You've never seen me smoking my corn-cob pipe anywhere else,' I explained, 'because I *keep* it in the hut all the time, safely hidden away. Usually – down on the beach, I mean, and so on – I smoke my ordinary pipe, the old one my uncle gave me, though now I've got this new one. But I've never taken the corn-cob pipe back home from the wood, not since I bought it. When did you last see me smoke it?'

Specs screwed his eyes up thoughtfully behind his glasses.

'I don't think I've seen you smoke your corn-cob pipe since the evening we celebrated getting the hut finished.'

'No, Specs,' I agreed, '*you* haven't seen me smoke it since then. But what about the others?'

'You were smoking it the night we

buried the treasure,' Katya remembered. 'I don't remember anything else, though.'

'There's nothing else *to* remember,' I explained. 'I've only ever smoked it those two times! And the first time we were all inside the hut, so no one else could have seen us.'

'I'm beginning to get the idea!' cried Erik. 'Well, blow me down! This is fantastic!'

The others looked at him inquiringly, and then at me, and then back at him again.

'Come on, out with it, what's the great explanation?' asked Specs.

'Listen!' said Erik excitedly. 'You see, Kim and I have been talking to someone who's seen that corn-cob pipe!'

'Hang on!' said Specs. 'You mean, that shows that person must be the thief? I see! Or rather, we can be almost certain he's the thief! Who is it?'

'Laursen!' I replied.

'The nasty, cunning rat!' muttered Erik

in disgust. 'So it must be him setting the snares too! Stands to reason. And today he swore blind he never went into the wood! That was when Larsen asked him if he knew about our hut, and he said no. And *that* was a lie, for a start!'

'And why would he lie about that if he had a clear conscience?' I said.

'Conscience!' said Erik. 'He wouldn't know what a conscience is!! Well, now what?'

'Catch him!' said Specs.

The Man from the Wood laughed. 'I'd like to be there when you do!' he chuckled. 'Mind, sonny, I don't think you'll bring it off, not on your own. Better let the police do the job. But leave me out of it, mind. The police hereabouts aren't too fond of the likes of me.'

Erik looked disappointed. 'I'd much rather catch him ourselves and *then* hand him over to the police!'

'Let's leave it till tonight,' I said. 'I expect I'll think of something by then.

Suppose we go home now and meet in Specs's lab at eight this evening.'

We got up and said goodbye to Mr Svensen. He said we were to let him know if we needed help, because he'd really like to get his hands on the fellow setting those traps. So we thanked him, and went home.

It was a lovely sunny evening as I walked to Specs's lab, later. The kind of evening when all the holidaymakers in a seaside place are out and about, walking along the harbour front to admire the sunset, and everything is warm and cheerful. There wasn't a breath of wind. If you stood still you could hear a record player somewhere in the distance, and motor boats starting up and going out into the bay. Everything was calm and peaceful – except for the fact that we were after a criminal, and determined to get him! It was a little after eight already, though, and I still hadn't thought of anything. I'd met the local policeman, Larsen, on the way, and he had called me over and told me that the police investigating the cause of the fire at High Farm had closed their case. It really was lightning that started it. He gave me a friendly slap on the back, and said he for one had never thought Erik and I were to blame, and I'm sure he meant it. I asked him what Laursen had said, and he replied that he hadn't set eyes on Laursen since midday. The way he said it indicated pretty clearly that he hadn't got much time for Laursen himself. I felt an urge to tell him it was Laursen who had been poaching and setting those traps, but I managed to keep my mouth shut.

I strolled slowly along, stopping frequently, trying to drag out the time. After all, there was no real hurry, since I didn't have any plan to put to the others. But at last I got there. The door was closed. I knocked, using our own signal, and went in. The other three were there already.

'Hi,' said Erik. 'Well, thought of anything?'

I shook my head. 'All I can think of is

going to his house and shadowing him when he goes out, but that's not what you'd call an ingenious plan. In fact, it's downright boring.'

'Yes, I thought of something like that,' Specs said. 'But you can't get close to that house without being seen. Maybe we could get somewhere by using my father's field-glasses . . . they're quite strong, and I've already got permission to borrow them. Only we'll have to be very careful not go get any sand in them. We could take them and lie in ambush some way away from the house.'

'OK, then, if that's the best we can think of, we'd better get moving!' said Erik. 'How about bringing your finger-printing equipment, Specs?'

'Got it here!' laughed Specs proudly, patting his pocket. 'And a torch too.'

So off we went.

We settled down to wait behind some bushes, field-glasses at the ready, looking across at Laursen's house and hoping he would go out. Of course, if he did we didn't know just what we intended to do next; our plans were very vague. We waited and waited. It was beginning to get dark, and we saw a light go on inside the house, but there was no indication that Laursen meant to go out.

'If only we could get into that shed of his!' muttered Erik. 'Maybe we'd find something in there that would prove he'd stolen the money. Or a trap. Or anyway, something with his finger-prints on it. Then we could compare them with the thief's prints.'

'Right!' said Katya, and she slipped off. We tried to call her back, but she didn't hear us. She disappeared from view behind some bushes, and we couldn't see her for some time. We kept the field-glasses trained on Laursen's house until she came into sight again, and then disappeared once more.

We lay there with bated breath, taking turns to look through the field-glasses. It had got so dark now that it was harder and harder to see anything at all. There was a lark singing high up in the sky above the field. It seemed to us as if the only sounds in the whole world were the lark's song and our own breathing.

Then Katya came back, emerging from the bushes as swiftly and silently as she had gone. She was holding something which she put down on the ground at our feet.

'This was the best I could do,' she whispered. 'Do you think it's a trap? There were three or four other things like it lying about in his shed.'

'Yes, that's a trap all right!'

Specs started taking finger-prints at once. We squatted round him, watching intently and driving off the midges; there were swarms of them round us by now. Unfortunately, Specs had no luck. He couldn't find any prints clear enough to take, and finally we gave up the attempt.

'Now what?' we wondered.

We sat there in silence for a long time,

thinking, and killing midges. It was as if our brains had just given up working. Then I suddenly had an idea. As my ideas go, it was a bit far-fetched, but the more I thought about it the better I liked it.

However, I don't want to boast, because to be perfectly honest it wasn't all my own idea. I'd seen something similar in a film last winter, a Western, and then – in the film, I mean – it had worked perfectly. I thought perhaps it might not work so well in real life, because after all, I'm not a cowboy, and Laursen was not an Indian, and naturally the details weren't all the same. However, it was the best I could manage to think of at the moment.

'I know!' I said decisively. 'We'll creep up to his house. It's dark enough to do that now. Then you three keep watching his windows, quite close, as close as you can get. You can divide up and each watch a different window. If he lets down blinds or anything, you'll just have to peep through the cracks. I'm not dead sure this will work, but it's our only chance. Erik, you can climb that tree beside the house – then you'll be able to see right in through the window of the first floor room.'

I handed him the field-glasses. 'And then what?' he asked, taking them. 'What do you expect us to see?'

'I think that you'll see where he's hidden the thousand *kroner*,' I said.

'I don't get it,' said Specs. 'How do you know he'll be hiding the thousand *kroner* just at the very moment we're watching him?'

'Because I'm going to persuade him to do it!' I replied. 'That's where my idea comes in. Come on, let's move.'

Of course, they still didn't understand my plan, but they obeyed and went with me. We walked down to the house, very quietly. Finally we were outside it; we saw that, like most people in the country, Laursen didn't bother with blinds in his windows. There was a light on in a room on the ground floor, and another in the first floor room. Erik climbed the tree beside the house, and whispered down to us, 'He's sitting in the room up here, reading the paper. Shall I stay here?'

'Yes! Something's going to happen pretty soon – at least, I hope so! Keep perfectly still, all three of you. And keep your eyes skinned!'

Specs and Katya took up their observation posts behind the bushes and the wooden fence. I took a deep breath to give myself courage, because I'll admit I was feeling rather nervous. Everything had gone so quiet all of a sudden. I heard a dog barking a long way off. Then I pulled myself together and prepared for action. I picked up some gravel and earth with one hand and threw it against the first floor window. Net result: nil. Far away, a long way off, down at the harbour maybe, I heard a girl laugh. I picked up another handful of gravel, with some larger pebbles in it this time, and threw that. This time it worked.

Laursen appeared, throwing up the window and putting his head out. I could see him straining his eyes to see in the dark. He hadn't spotted me yet, though I was right below him.

'What's all this in aid of, eh?' he shouted.

'Good evening, Mr Laursen,' I said, trying to keep my voice perfectly steady. I wasn't entirely successful. 'It's me, Kim, I just wanted to let you know I've discovered that it was you who dug up our treasure and took the money. I made a note of the numbers of the bank-notes. So now I'd like them back, please.'

'Are you quite out of your mind?' he asked.

'No, not at all. I just want my money back! If I don't get it, I'm going straight down to fetch the police. So you might as well give it back now.'

'You poor, deluded boy!' he said sarcastically. 'Off you go, then – fetch the police, if you dare!'

'You bet I dare! All right, then, that's what I'll do. I'm off to fetch the police now. Be seeing you!'

I turned and left. I walked along the road to the village, whistling to myself so that he could hear I really was going away. I knew he'd be standing by the open window listening to my footsteps. I went all the way to the wood and a little further, taking care to make as much noise as possible the whole time.

When I thought I'd gone far enough, I took to the soft grass verge and ran back the same way I'd come.

Erik came to meet me, grinning all over his face, and I had to tell him to keep his voice down.

'Kim, this is terrific! He fell into the trap!'

'And where was the money?' I asked.

'In his desk drawer. As soon as you'd gone he rushed to the drawer and took the money out. The desk's in that first floor room, so I could see everything through the field-glasses. Then he stood there for a moment, looking round the room. I could see he was wondering where he could hide the notes so the police wouldn't find them. Finally he went downstairs to the ground floor with them – and Katya and Specs saw the rest!'

'Where did he hide them?'

'In a very clever place. He put them in an old newspaper, crumpled it all up and put it in the tiled stove, among some other bits of waste paper which were there already. Then he emptied some ashtrays over the lot, and after that he went back to the first floor room and calmly sat down and went on reading the paper. He's still sitting there, waiting for you to come back with Larsen.'

By this time Katya had joined us. Specs had climbed the tree to keep an eye on Laursen.

'Now what?' asked Katya. 'How do we get him to leave the house?'

'I'll see to that,' I told her. 'At least, I

hope I will! You two wait here, and don't take your eyes off him till I come back. If he goes out, follow him, but very carefully. Only two of you – Specs and Erik, for choice, and Katya can wait here to let me know. So long!'

Chapter 8

I started off towards the village again. I walked until I reached the first cluster of villas and holiday houses. One of these houses belonged to a family I'd visited once or twice with my aunt and uncle. There was a light on in their house, so I went in at the garden gate, rang the bell, and asked if I could use their phone. The people were very nice and helpful; they had guests in, so they just showed me the room where the telephone was and left me to it. I looked up Laursen's number in the telephone book and rang it. He answered the phone at once.

'Good evening, Mr Laursen,' I said. 'This is Kim again. I can't get hold of Larsen tonight, but if I don't get the money back by tomorrow morning I'm going to report you! And I'll tell them you've been setting snares in the wood, too! The police are sure to find fingerprints on all your traps. Good night!'

I put the receiver down, chuckling to myself. If he fell for that one, he wasn't so clever as I'd thought!

I thanked the owners of the house for letting me use their phone, and went back to Laursen's place. Someone was just leaving the house. I couldn't see who it was, so I hid behind a bush and waited. No more than seven or eight minutes could have passed since I rang up – could this be Laursen already? Yes, it was! I lay perfectly still behind the bush, watched him go past in the direction of the wood, and very nearly gave three loud cheers. However, I managed to keep quiet and stayed where I was. I knew Specs and Erik would be following him, and I didn't want to frighten them, in case they lost track of him. I waited till they were right beside me, and then emerged from my hiding place.

'Was it you phoning?' whispered Erik. 'What did you say to him?'

I grinned. 'Tell you later! He'll be on his way to the wood to clear all his traps away now. You two go after him. Katya and I will follow – if we can find you, that is.'

'Wait a moment,' Specs whispered. 'I've got a little notepad here. I'll tear scraps of paper off and scatter them behind us in the wood, to help you follow the trail.'

'Good idea,' I said. They went on, following Laursen, who was well ahead by this time, and I ran back to the house, where I found Katya. We set to work at once. First I tried both doors of the house, but they were locked. So we went all round the house trying the windows, but they were all fastened. However, then Katya spotted a first floor window still open – the one where Laursen had stood to talk to me. Well, not really open, but not quite closed.

We found a ladder and put it up to the

window, but it was not long enough. We fetched a garden table and stood the ladder on that. Now it was just the right length, though the whole contraption was rather wobbly. We decided that I'd stay at the bottom and hold the thing steady, while Katya cautiously climbed the ladder. When she was nearly at the top it began to slip, but I put all my weight against it, and finally she got hold of the window frame.

'Katya . . . wait a minute,' I called up softly.

'What for?'

'I don't know . . . I don't quite like all this.'

'What do you mean, "all this"?'

'Climbing into his house.'

'Whyever not, Kim?'

'It's just . . . I mean . . . well, it's kind of breaking and entering, isn't it? I suppose it's against the law, doing this kind of thing.'

'But why? It's our own money we're after!' she said indignantly.

'That doesn't make any difference,' I objected. I didn't really feel too good about this at all; in fact, I suddenly wanted to give the whole idea up.

'You listen to me!' Katya whispered. 'If someone steals our money and hides it in his house, haven't we got a right to go in and get it back?'

'I don't know, Katya. No, I don't think we have.'

'Then what are we supposed to do?' she asked.

'Well, we really ought to go and tell the police and leave the rest to them.'

'But think of all the trouble we're saving the police by doing the job ourselves!' she said.

'Yes, but that's not the point. The law is the law!'

'Who says so?'

'My father.'

'Huh!' she said scornfully. 'You men! You think laws are more important than anything else!'

I rather liked the way she said 'You men', but I was just going to point out where she was wrong, when she went on, 'If we tell the police, they'll search the house and then give us back the money, won't they?'

'Yes, I should think so,' I agreed.

'And Laursen will go to prison. But if we climb in and get our own money back for ourselves, then we *know* we've got it, and we get it much quicker, and Laursen doesn't have to go to prison – at least, not because of the money. And the police can get a good night's sleep too! Honestly, sometimes I think laws are just stupid!'

With which statement she put her foot on the top rung of the ladder, and wriggled in through the window.

So I was left standing there. But I decided I'd have to discuss this whole thing properly with Katya, later, and try to make her see the error of her ways.

After a minute or so she opened the door and softly called me in. It was dark.

She took my hand and led me through a passage and into a room. She let go of my hand and began to root around in the stove.

'Here we are!' she said triumphantly, unfolding a crumpled newspaper. She held the money out to me. I counted it. All ten of my hundred *kroner* notes! Nothing had happened to them; they were just a bit creased. It was a wonderful feeling to have them in my hands again.

Katya stuffed the newspaper back in the stove and closed the little door. Now no one could see that it had been touched. Then we left the house, pulling the door shut behind us so as to lock it, and began to walk away.

'Let's sit down here a moment,' I said. We sat down on the wet grass, and I took out the money and handed it to Katya. Then I looked for the piece of paper where I'd written down the numbers of the notes.

'I'll read out the numbers,' I suggested, 'and you can check them off against the notes.'

I began. 'M 671 2724?' Katya searched around and found the note. 'Yes,' she said. I went on, 'M 671 2725?' 'Yes. Look, you don't need to call them all out like that" she said. 'They're in numerical order; I've just sorted them out. M 671 2726–7–8–9–30–31–32–33. Yes, it's our money all right. But we knew that all along!'

'I know, but it's nice to be sure,' I said, relieved. I put the money in my back trouser pocket, and buttoned it up so that the notes couldn't fall out. Then we went over to the wood. I told Katya about the scraps of paper Specs was going to scatter, and soon we found the first of them, right at the start of one of the paths leading through the wood. I felt sure Laursen would be well inside the wood by now, so I thought it was safe to switch the torch on. It was quite easy to follow the trail of paper by torchlight; it led us deeper and deeper into the wood. We went cautiously, but we made quite good speed.

Then I heard something. I stopped

dead, and so did Katya, just behind me. I could hear her heart thumping.

'Ssh! It's only me!' Erik emerged from the shadows. 'Specs is still after him. Listen – he's chasing all over the place, collecting his snares, so all we have to do is wait for him. There's a trap close to the place where we were sitting today. I fixed it with Specs that we'd go there and hide. Specs has told me just where it is.'

I thought this was a good idea, and about ten minutes later we found the place, without too much trouble. We examined the trap. It was a sort of fox-trap with horrible, pointed, rusty teeth. I felt sorry for any animal that got caught in that! We lay down and waited, and as time went by, and we had nothing to do but stare at that trap, which was in full view, we felt angrier and angrier with the person who had set it.

We waited for half an hour, during which time we hardly spoke a word. We were all feeling very indignant about that trap; we took it out on the midges, which just wouldn't leave us alone and were biting like mad. Still, they couldn't really help it. At the end of half an hour we heard Laursen coming. We lay flat on the ground and let the midges do their worst.

He didn't switch his torch on until he was right beside the trap, bending down to snap it shut. He couldn't see us, but I was afraid he'd be able to hear my heart beating. And I suddenly realized I had no idea what we were going to do next.

But suddenly a great many things happened all at once. Erik started it by jumping up and flinging himself on Laursen. 'Get him!' he cried.

Laursen had dropped the torch. I jumped on him from behind and wrapped my arms round his neck, and we all three fell to the ground. I was afraid one of us might get an arm or leg caught in that trap, because Erik had attacked Laursen before he could put the mechanism out of action. We had a terrific fight. None of us spoke a word, we just fought desperately, in silence. I'd never have thought I had that much strength! Then Specs came crashing through the bushes. He'd heard the noise and was coming to help us. Katya did her bit too; she tugged at Laursen's legs, which wasn't really much help, but she meant well. So now we were four against one. He was carrying a rope over his shoulder, with the traps he'd already collected hanging from it. I let go of him and tried to grab the rope. This was a mistake, because when I let go of him he managed to break free, and Erik and Specs, who weren't expecting me to loosen my grip, were flung off into the grass on either side of him. So there I sat with nothing but the rope in my hands; it had only been loosely thrown over his shoulder, so that he could just shake it off and run away through the thick undergrowth. His torch lay beside the trap, still switched on. I cursed myself. What a fool I'd been!

'After him!' shouted Erik. He was up on

his feet in a moment, giving chase. Specs and I followed. Katya came after us, with the rope and the torch, dragging the traps along as she tried to keep up. However, they kept getting caught on things, so she soon fell behind. We couldn't see very well, but we used the sound of Laursen's running footsteps to guide us, and suddenly we heard him let out a yell. We ran as fast as we could, but I think we all knew at once what that yell meant: Laursen had run straight into the arms of the Man from the Wood, our friendly tramp, *Mister* Svensen, as Specs had called him.

It was an edifying moment, I assure you! We came up and stood round in a circle to enjoy the fight. Soon Katya came panting up, traps and all, and joined us.

Our Mr Svensen had a broad grin on his face; he looked as if he enjoyed a good fight. Laursen, on the other hand, didn't look as if he liked it at all.

'You just wait a moment, lads!' said

Svensen. 'Your turn soon! I've got a bone to pick with him first, though.'

He lowered his head, ready to wade in. Laursen took a swing at him, but Svensen's fist caught him hard, just where it hurt. Svensen grinned. 'That's from a little squirrel I found in one of your traps the other day. And here's some more of the same! How d'you like that, you brute?'

Laursen didn't seem to like it one little bit. He collapsed on the ground, shielding his head with his arms. Mr Svensen stopped. He stood there for a moment, panting slightly, and then, noticing the rope Katya was holding, he took it from her.

A few moments later Laursen was lying on the ground, bound hand and foot. He had hardly resisted at all when Svensen tied him up. The knots were pretty tight, and they must have been hurting his wrists, but it was difficult to feel sorry for him once you'd seen those traps.

'Well, I reckon you can manage on your

own now,' said our tramp. 'Good night. And look, don't you go mentioning me to the police, there's good kids. Not if you can help it, that is. Never mind if you can't. I've got nothing to hide. I just want to be left alone.'

'Good night,' said Katya. 'And thank you very much for helping us.'

We heard him making his way through the bushes. 'Got the money, Kim?' Erik asked.

I took it out of my pocket and handed it to him. He grinned and counted the notes. Then he handed them to Specs. Laursen was lying on the ground tied up all this time, staring at us, but he didn't say a word.

Then Erik went off to the village to fetch the police. By this time Laursen had begun to beg us to let him go, but we were all furious with him because of his horrible traps. However, I told him we wouldn't say anything about the thousand *kroner* so long as he didn't mention them himself.

At last Erik came back with Larsen and one of the other policemen who had come to get us at midday. They untied Laursen's legs, and then we all left the wood together, with Laursen in between the two policemen and the rest of us bringing up the rear, taking turns to carry the traps.

The police car was waiting on the main road. The policemen shoved Laursen into the back seat and slammed the doors. Then Larsen turned to us and made what was practically a speech. We could tell how glad he was to have got the man who had been setting those traps. He told us we'd have to go to court tomorrow and make a statement, and then he said thank you and wished us good night.

We stood there feeling very limp and tired all of a sudden, watching the red rear lights of the police car disappear into the dark.

Finally we shook off our lethargy and went slowly back to the fishing village. It was a still night, and we were quiet too.

I had the odd feeling that the whole thing had been only a dream; I had to force myself to believe it was only twenty-four hours ago we'd discovered the loss of our treasure. And now we had it back again! It was sitting in Specs's breast pocket, and Specs kept his hand pressed on it the whole time.

'I've never known so many things to happen in a single day!' murmured Erik. 'Well, what are we going to do next?'

I had to laugh. 'Haven't you had enough?' But I knew what he meant.

'Listen, do you really think I ought to use this money for my invention?' Specs asked, rather abruptly.

'Well, of course! Let's all go and see Stoffer tomorrow. He'll know what you need to get first.'

'Thanks,' said Specs, awkwardly. 'Well . . . well, thanks! You just don't know . . .'

He stopped, looking so solemn I feared the worst.

'Careful, Specs – don't get all worked

up!' said Erik anxiously, and we all laughed.

We went on in the direction of home. Now we were all talking nineteen to the dozen again, making plans for the rest of the holidays. Suddenly we realized what a lot of holidays we still had left. Any amount of things could happen before term began again! Somehow, we'd acquired a taste for exciting adventures; we thought it would be nice to have some more.

We felt more and more cheerful, and our voices got louder and louder. The moon had risen, and we made a détour so as to go down to the beach. The water shone like silver, and the stars were twinkling in the sky. We walked along the deserted beach, feeling the whole world belonged just to us. We were quite dizzy at the prospect of all that holiday ahead.

A dog came running up to us. It was Schnapp. He jumped up at us, quite beside himself with pleasure, and we threw bits of wood into the water for him to retrieve.

'Show us the money again, Specs!' Katya said.

He took it out of his pocket, and we all four stood there for a few moments, with our heads together, looking at those precious notes in the moonlight.

Then Schnapp got impatient, and Specs put the money away again. We said good night to each other down at the harbour.

'Let's meet at eight-thirty tomorrow morning in Specs's lab – OK?' I suggested.

I went back to my uncle's house. What a night! I opened the door quietly and crept upstairs to my room. I got undressed, and went to bed, but I couldn't sleep, because the moon was shining in at my window so brightly. Anyway, I didn't feel like going to sleep. So I got up again, and found some paper, and began to write the whole story down.

I heard a fishing boat out at sea; I stopped writing to listen to the sound. It grew fainter and fainter, until finally it died away to the north-east, far out in the Kattegat.